Veggie Burritos

Preparing this vegetarian burrito recipe for kids is easy! Start by cooking the cilantro-lime rice according to package instructions. Meanwhile, heat a large skillet over medium-high heat and add oil. When hot, add black beans that have been seasoned with chipotle spice. Cook until heated through and beginning to char, stirring occasionally. Next, add peppers and onions to the pan and cook until softened, about 5 minutes more.

To make the avocado cream sauce, prepare it in a food processor by adding avocado, cilantro, jalapeño, garlic, lime juice and either sour cream or Greek yogurt. Process until fully combined before removing from heat and stirring in 3 Tbsp of water for desired consistency.

Once all components of the vegetarian burrito are ready, have kids help assemble their creation. This recipe is great for vegetarian recipes for kids and healthy recipes they can create themselves! Enjoy!

An easy lunch recipes cookbook is a compilation of simple and delicious meal ideas that are perfect for anyone looking for quick and hassle-free lunch options. This cookbook features a variety of recipes that can be made in under 30 minutes, using basic ingredients that are easily available at your local grocery store.

The cookbook offers a range of options to cater to different tastes and dietary preferences, including vegetarian, vegan, and gluten-free recipes. From sandwiches, wraps, salads, and soups to pasta dishes, rice bowls, and stir-fries, this cookbook has something for everyone.

Each recipe in the cookbook is accompanied by clear and easy-to-follow instructions, along with a list of ingredients and nutritional information. The cookbook also includes tips and tricks for meal prepping, making substitutions, and adjusting portion sizes to suit your needs.

Whether you're a busy professional, a student, or a parent looking for quick and easy lunch ideas, this cookbook is the perfect solution. With its simple yet delicious recipes, you'll be able to whip up tasty and nutritious meals in no time, leaving you more time to enjoy your lunch break.

Chicken Fried Rice

Chicken Fried Rice is a delicious, easy and fast meal that you can prepare in minutes. It's one of the most popular chicken recipes around, and it's easy to see why! This comfort food dish packs plenty of flavor and nutrition all into one easy-to-make meal.

The ingredients in Chicken Fried Rice are simple, but the flavors are anything but. Start by heating oil (both sesame and vegetable) in a wok or large skillet over medium-high heat. Once hot, add chicken breasts and sauté until cooked through. Add frozen peas and carrots, green onions, garlic, eggs and cooked rice to the pan and cook until everything is heated through. Finally, stir in low-sodium soy sauce for some added flavor and serve.

With just a few simple ingredients and easy steps, you can have a delicious meal ready to go in no time! So next time you're looking for an easy and flavorful chicken recipe, give Chicken Fried Rice a try - it's sure to be a hit!

Happy cooking!

Penne Arrabiata

Ingredients
6 tablespoons extra virgin olive oil, plus extra for cooking the pasta
2 medium hot chilies, finely sliced
2 garlic cloves, chopped
Handful of basil leaves
600g/1lb 5oz canned chopped tomatoes
Salt, to taste
400g/14oz fresh penne pasta
Parmesan shavings (or similar vegetarian hard cheese), to serve

Instructions:

Heat the olive oil in a large saucepan over medium heat.

Add the sliced chilies and chopped garlic to the pan and sauté for 1-2 minutes, stirring frequently, until the garlic is fragrant.

Add the canned chopped tomatoes to the pan and bring to a simmer. Cook the sauce for 10-15 minutes, stirring occasionally, until it has thickened slightly.

While the sauce is cooking, bring a large pot of salted water to a boil. Add the fresh penne pasta and cook according to package instructions until al dente.

Reserve a cup of the pasta cooking water and then drain the penne.

Add the cooked penne to the saucepan with the arrabiata sauce and toss well to coat the pasta in the sauce. If the sauce seems too thick, add a splash of the reserved pasta cooking water to loosen it up.

Season the Penne Arrabiata with salt to taste.

Serve the Penne Arrabiata in bowls, topped with fresh basil leaves and Parmesan shavings. Enjoy!

Crispy Potato Tacos

INGREDIENTS

2 LARGE RUSSET POTATOES.
¾ CUP SOUR CREAM.
2 CLOVES GARLIC, MINCED.
½ TEASPOON CUMIN.
SALT, TO TASTE.
½ TEASPOON OREGANO.
8 CORN TORTILLAS.
OIL, FOR FRYING.

Crispy potato tacos are a healthy vegetarian recipe for kids that is easy to prepare. Start by preheating your oven to 400°F and scrubbing the potatoes clean. Cut them into thin slices, about ¼-inch thick, and place onto a baking sheet lined with parchment paper. Drizzle with oil and sprinkle with salt, then bake for 25 minutes or until golden brown.

While the potatoes are baking, make the sour cream garlic sauce by combining the sour cream, minced garlic, cumin, oregano and salt in a bowl. Mix ingredients until everything is well combined.

Once the potatoes have finished baking, heat up some oil in a large skillet over high heat. Place four of the tortillas in the skillet and cook for 30-45 seconds per side until lightly browned. Place them on a plate lined with paper towels to absorb any excess oil.

To assemble tacos, place two potato slices inside each tortilla, then top with some of the sour cream garlic sauce and fold in half. Repeat this process with the remaining four tortillas and serve immediately. Enjoy!

These vegetarian crispy potato tacos are sure to be a hit amongst kids and adults alike! So next time you're looking for an easy, healthy vegetarian recipe for kids, try making these delicious tacos. They'll definitely make dinner time much more fun!

Creamy Mushroom Pasta

Ingredients

8 ounces fettuccine pasta.
2 tablespoons olive oil.
¾ pound fresh white mushrooms, sliced.
¼ pound fresh shiitake mushrooms, stemmed and sliced.
salt and ground black pepper to taste.
2 cloves garlic, minced.
2 fluid ounces sherry.
1 cup chicken stock.

If you're looking for delicious recipes for kids, this creamy mushroom pasta is sure to please. With just a few ingredients and some simple steps, you can have an amazing dinner on your table in no time!

To start, bring a large pot of lightly salted water to a boil over high heat. Add the fettuccine pasta and cook for 8 to 10 minutes, or until al dente. Drain the pasta and set aside.

Next, heat the olive oil in a large skillet over medium-high heat. Add the mushrooms, season with salt and pepper, and sauté for 5 minutes. Reduce the heat to low, add the garlic and sherry, and cook for another 2 minutes.

Finally, add the chicken stock and bring to a boil. Once boiling, reduce heat to low and simmer for 5 minutes. Add the cooked fettuccine pasta and stir until the sauce coats the noodles evenly. Serve warm and enjoy!

This delicious mushroom pasta is sure to be a hit with kids of all ages. With its creamy sauce and delicious mushrooms, it's sure to become a family favorite. So don't wait any longer - try this delicious recipe today!

Bon Appétit!

Crispy Black Bean And Sweet Potato Tacos

Ingredients
8-10 tortillas (see notes)
2 14 oz can black beans, drained.
2 sweet potatoes, diced (skin on or peeled)
1 Tablespoon oil.
1/2 teaspoon (each) cumin, paprika, chili powder.
1/2 teaspoon garlic powder.
salt to taste.

These vegetarian black bean and sweet potato tacos are an easy, healthy, and delicious way to get your kids eating vegetarian! They can be made in under 30 minutes with very few ingredients - perfect for busy nights. To prepare, simply heat up the oil in a large skillet over medium-high heat. Add in the diced sweet potatoes and season with cumin, paprika, chili powder, garlic powder and salt. Cook until the potatoes are soft (about 10 minutes). Then add in the drained black beans and cook for another 2-3 minutes until everything is heated through.

To assemble the tacos grab 8-10 tortillas (or however many you like) spread some of the mixture on each taco shell then top with your favorite toppings like shredded cheese, tomatoes, lettuce, or salsa. Enjoy!

These vegetarian tacos are a great way to get your kids eating healthier and trying new vegetarian recipes. They're easy to make, full of flavor, and customizable with whatever toppings you have on hand. Give these vegetarian black bean and sweet potato tacos a try for your next vegetarian dinner! Your family will love them.

Baked Potato Bar

Ingredients

5 pounds baked potatoes.
3-5 pounds pulled pork cooked.
2 cups sharp cheddar cheese shredded.
1/2 pound bacon cooked & crumbled.
1 cup sour cream.
1/2 cup chives chopped.
2 cups broccoli cooked.
1 bottle bbq sauce.

A baked potato bar is an easy and healthy dinner option for kids, and it's simple to prepare. Start by baking five pounds of potatoes according to the instructions on the package. While they're cooking, pre-cook three to five pounds of pulled pork as well as one-half pound of bacon. Once the potatoes are done, split them open and sprinkle two cups of shredded sharp cheddar cheese over the top. Then, add the cooked pulled pork, crumbled bacon, one cup of sour cream, half a cup of chopped chives and two cups of cooked broccoli. Finally, make sure to provide some BBQ sauce for everyone to enjoy. With minimal effort, you can create a delicious and nutritious baked potato bar that all the kids will love! Enjoy!

Chicken Tortellini

Ingredients

2 tablespoons olive oil.
8 oz boneless skinless chicken breast, cut into 1/4-inch slices.
3 cups fresh small broccoli florets.
2 teaspoons chopped garlic.
1 1/2 cups Progresso™ chicken broth (from 32-oz carton)
2 packages (9 oz each) refrigerated cheese tortellini.
1 cup milk.

Preparing a healthy and easy dinner for the kids doesn't have to be a hassle. This delicious Chicken Tortellini is sure to please everyone at the table.

To make this dish, start by heating two tablespoons of olive oil in a large skillet over medium-high heat. Once it's hot, add the chicken slices and cook for about 4 minutes until they're no longer pink. Add the broccoli florets, garlic, and a pinch of salt, then cook for another 3 to 4 minutes.

Next, pour in the Progresso™ chicken broth and bring it to a boil over high heat. Once boiling, add the tortellini and cook for about 8 minutes until the pasta is cooked through. Then, reduce the heat to low and stir in the milk. Simmer for a few more minutes until it thickens up a bit. Taste and season with salt and pepper if needed.

Serve the tortellini with some extra grated Parmesan cheese on top. Enjoy! This Chicken Tortellini is a healthy and delicious dinner that your kids are sure to love. It's quick and easy, ready in just 30 minutes. Enjoy!

*Note: You can customize this dish with other vegetables like mushrooms, bell peppers or spinach. For added protein, you can also add shrimp or cooked sausage. Enjoy!

Enjoy! With its delicious flavor and simple preparation, this Chicken Tortellini is a surefire winner for any family dinner. It's the perfect healthy and easy dinner for kids - ready in just 30 minutes! Bon appetit!

Pulled Chicken Salad

1 small roasted chicken, about 1kg
½ red cabbage, cored and finely sliced
3 carrots, coarsely grated or finely shredded
5 spring onions, finely sliced on the diagonal
2 red chillies, halved and thinly sliced
A small bunch of coriander, roughly chopped, including stalks

Instructions for preparing Pulled Chicken Salad:

Remove the meat from the roasted chicken and shred it into bite-sized pieces using two forks or your hands.

In a large bowl, mix together the shredded chicken, finely sliced red cabbage, grated carrots, finely sliced spring onions, thinly sliced red chillies, and chopped coriander.

Season the salad with salt and pepper, to taste.

To serve, arrange the salad on a large platter or divide it evenly onto individual plates. You can also drizzle some vinaigrette or your favorite dressing over the salad, if desired.

Serve the Pulled Chicken Salad immediately and enjoy!

Lemon Mushroom Chicken

Ingredients:

4 chicken breasts (about 3/4 pound total)
1 1/2 tbsp unsalted butter, divided
8 oz cremini mushrooms, sliced
1/4 tsp salt
1/2 cup dry sherry
1/4 cup lemon juice
1/2 cup heavy cream
2 1/2 cups baby spinach

Instructions:

Season the chicken breasts with salt and pepper.

In a large pan, heat 1 tbsp of butter over medium heat. Add the chicken breasts and cook for about 4-5 minutes on each side, or until golden brown and fully cooked. Remove the chicken from the pan and set aside.

In the same pan, add the remaining butter and sliced mushrooms. Cook the mushrooms for about 4-5 minutes, or until they are tender and lightly browned.

Add the sherry to the pan and use a wooden spoon to scrape the bottom of the pan to release any browned bits. Cook the sherry for about 2 minutes, or until it has reduced by half.

Add the lemon juice and heavy cream to the pan and stir to combine. Cook the sauce for about 2-3 minutes, or until it has thickened slightly.

Return the chicken breasts to the pan and add the baby spinach. Stir to combine and cook for about 2 minutes, or until the spinach has wilted.

Serve the chicken with the lemon mushroom sauce on top. Enjoy!

Vegan Mac And Cheese

Vegan mac and cheese is a vegetarian-friendly take on the classic dish that kids love. It's an easy, healthy recipe that can be quickly prepared any night of the week. To make vegan mac and cheese, you'll need 1 1/2 cups raw cashews, 2 cups water, 3 tablespoons fresh lemon juice, 1/2 cup nutritional yeast, 1/4 teaspoon turmeric, 1/2 teaspoon garlic powder and 1 1/2 teaspoons salt. For vegetarian recipes for kids, you can also add a 7-oz bag of shredded vegan cheddar cheese for extra flavor.

To prepare your vegan mac and cheese: first combine the cashews with the water in a blender or food processor until smooth. Next add the lemon juice, nutritional yeast, turmeric, garlic powder and salt. Blend until creamy and smooth.

Pour the mixture into a pot and cook over medium-high heat while stirring constantly. Once the sauce has thickened, remove it from heat and stir in the shredded cheese if using. Serve warm with your favorite vegetarian sides like steamed broccoli or edamame beans.

Vegan mac and cheese makes for a healthy recipe that kids will love as an alternative to traditional macaroni dishes. Enjoy!

Creamy Tomato Soup

Tomato Soup is a great lunch choice for kids because it's easy to make and packed with healthy ingredients. Plus, they will love the bright and vibrant colour! Here's what you'll need to make this delicious tomato soup recipe:

- 1-1.25kg/2lb 4oz-2lb 12oz ripe tomatoes
- 1 medium onion
- 1 small carrot
- 1 celery stick
- 2 tbsp olive oil
- 2 squirts of tomato purée (about 2 tsp)
- A good pinch of sugar
- 2 bay leaves

Once you've gathered all the ingredients, it's time to start cooking! Begin by heating the olive oil in a large saucepan and adding the diced onion, carrot, celery stick. Cook over medium heat for about 5 minutes until softened. Then add the tomatoes, purée, bay leaves and sugar. Cover with a lid and cook for 40 minutes. Once the soup is cooked, remove the bay leaves and blend until smooth with a blender.

Serve up this delicious tomato soup with some crusty bread or croutons on top and you have an easy, healthy lunch that your kids will love! Enjoy!

Spaghetti Alla Norma

Ingredients

2 aubergines (eggplants), cut into small cubes
3 cloves of garlic, minced
1/2 bunch of fresh basil (about 15g), finely chopped
1 teaspoon dried oregano
1 teaspoon dried chili flakes
Olive oil, for cooking
1 tablespoon baby capers
1 tablespoon red wine vinegar
1 x 400g can of quality plum tomatoes, crushed or pureed
320g dried wholewheat spaghetti
50g pecorino cheese, grated
Extra-virgin olive oil, for serving

Instructions:

Preheat your oven to 200°C (180°C fan)/400°F/gas 6.

Spread the cubed aubergines in a single layer on a baking tray, drizzle with olive oil and sprinkle with salt. Roast for 20-25 minutes until golden and tender.

In a large pan, heat 2-3 tablespoons of olive oil over medium heat. Add the minced garlic, dried oregano, and dried chili flakes, and cook for a minute until fragrant.

Add the baby capers and red wine vinegar to the pan and cook for another minute.

Pour in the crushed/pureed plum tomatoes and stir to combine with the garlic mixture. Bring the sauce to a simmer and let it cook for 10-15 minutes, stirring occasionally.

Cook the spaghetti according to the package instructions until al dente.

Drain the spaghetti, reserving 1/2 cup of the pasta cooking water.

Add the cooked spaghetti to the tomato sauce and toss to combine. If the sauce seems too thick, add a splash of the reserved pasta cooking water to loosen it up.

Add the roasted aubergines to the pan with the spaghetti and tomato sauce, and stir to combine.

Serve the Spaghetti alla Norma hot, topped with grated pecorino cheese and fresh chopped basil. Drizzle with extra-virgin olive oil before serving. Enjoy!

Pesto Pasta

Ingredients

6 ounces spaghetti, reserve 1/2 cup starchy pasta water.
1/3 to 1/2 cup. basil pesto or vegan pesto.
Extra-virgin olive oil, for drizzling.
Fresh lemon juice, as desired.
4 cups arugula.
2 tablespoons pine nuts.
Pinches of red pepper flakes.
Sea salt and freshly ground black pepper.

Pesto pasta is a great way to make a healthy, delicious lunch for the kids. Start by boiling your spaghetti in salted water according to the package instructions. Once cooked, reserve about 1/2 cup of starchy boiled pasta water before draining.

In a separate bowl, mix together basil pesto (or vegan pesto if desired) with a drizzle of extra-virgin olive oil, fresh lemon juice and some salt and freshly ground black pepper.

Toss the cooked spaghetti in the pesto mixture until everything is evenly coated. If the mixture looks too thick, add some starchy pasta water to thin it out.

Finally, top with a handful of arugula, some pine nuts and a pinch of red pepper flakes for an extra kick. Serve the pesto pasta warm or at room temperature - it's sure to be a hit! Enjoy!

For an even healthier version, swap out the spaghetti for your favorite whole grain variety or try zucchini noodles for a low-carb option. Top with tomatoes, olives or your favorite veggies to make it even more nutritious and tasty.
Happy eating!

Baked Fish

Here's a list of ingredients for a baked fish recipe:

White fish fillets
Cherry tomatoes
Red onion
Garlic
Green olives
Capers
Fresh parsley
Olive oil
Dried oregano
Lemon juice
Salt and pepper, to taste

Instructions:

Preheat the oven to 375°F (190°C).

Line a baking dish with parchment paper or lightly grease it with oil.

Rinse the fish fillets and pat them dry with paper towels. Place them in the prepared baking dish.

Slice the cherry tomatoes in half and arrange them around the fish fillets.

Thinly slice the red onion and scatter it over the tomatoes.

Mince the garlic and sprinkle it over the onions.

Add the green olives and capers to the dish.

Chop the fresh parsley and sprinkle it over the top of the fish.

Drizzle the dish with olive oil and sprinkle with dried oregano.

Squeeze the lemon juice over the dish and season with salt and pepper, to taste.

Bake the fish in the preheated oven for 20-25 minutes, or until the fish is opaque and flakes easily with a fork.

Serve the baked fish hot, garnished with additional chopped parsley, if desired. Enjoy!

Taco Pizza

NGREDIENTS

1 (12-16 OUNCE) PIZZA DOUGH, (DEPENDING ON IF YOU WANT THICK OR THIN CRUST)
1 LB GROUND BEEF.
1 (1 OUNCE) PACKET OF TACO SEASONING.
1 (15 OUNCE) CAN REFRIED BEANS.
1/4 CUP SALSA.
2 CUPS SHREDDED CHEDDAR CHEESE , (OR MEXICAN BLEND CHEESE)
SLICED OLIVES, (ABOUT 1/4 CUP)

Taco pizza is a delicious and easy meal to prepare. Start by preheating your oven to 375°F (190°C). To make the dough, roll out the pizza dough and place it onto a lightly greased baking sheet.

Next, cook the ground beef in a skillet over medium heat until browned. Once done, stir in the taco seasoning until combined. Spread the refried beans over the pizza crust, followed by the cooked ground beef. Top with salsa and cheese of your choice (cheddar or Mexican blend). Finally, top with sliced olives before baking for 20-25 minutes or until golden brown.

Once done, remove from oven and let cool for 5-10 minutes. Slice into pieces and enjoy your delicious taco pizza. With a few simple ingredients, you can create a delicious and savory meal in no time! Try out other delicious pizza recipes to satisfy your craving for something delicious. Bon Appetit!

Goat Cheese Pizza

Goat Cheese Pizza is a delicious recipe that is both easy to make and delicious to eat. This delicious pizza combines delicious ingredients like homemade pizza sauce, mozzarella cheese, soft goat cheese, red onion slices and oregano into a delicious combination that will have your family coming back for seconds!

To start off this delicious meal, you will need one recipe of either the Best Pizza Dough, Thin Crust Pizza Dough or Pizza Oven Dough. Once you have the dough prepared, spread ⅓ cup of Homemade Pizza Sauce on top. Then sprinkle ½ cup of shredded mozzarella cheese over top. Break up 3 ounces of soft goat cheese (chevre) and dot it around the pizza. Lastly add 1 handful of red onion slices and a sprinkle of ¼ teaspoon dried oregano. Finish off the pizza by adding some kosher salt and fresh ground black pepper to taste.

Once all your delicious ingredients are added, bake in an oven preheated to 500°F for 10-15 minutes or until the cheese is melted and bubbly. For a delicious finishing touch, garnish with some fresh basil leaves before serving.

Try this delicious Goat Cheese Pizza recipe tonight and enjoy delicious, easy-to-make pizza that's sure to be a hit! Enjoy!

Chicken Caesar Salad

If you want to make an easy and fast chicken caesar salad, then you've come to the right place! This recipe is easy to prepare, and uses simple ingredients that are easy to find. To start, chop 6 cups of tightly packed romaine lettuce and set aside. Next cook 1 pound of boneless skinless chicken breasts until cooked through, then cut into strips. In a bowl, mix together the chicken strips, lettuce and ½ cup of finely shredded parmesan cheese. Add in ½ cup of seasoned croutons and ¼ cup of creamy caesar dressing. Mix everything together and serve your easy and delicious chicken caesar salad! For more easy-to-make chicken recipes, check out our website for more ideas. Enjoy!

Creamy Salmon Pasta

Ingredients
2 salmon fillets.
1 tbsp olive oil, plus 1 tsp if roasting.
175g penne.
2 shallots or 1 small onion, finely chopped.
1 garlic clove, crushed.
100ml white wine.
200ml double cream or crème fraîche.
¼ lemon, zested and juiced.

Creamy salmon pasta is a delicious and easy recipe for kids. This delicious meal can be prepared in just a few simple steps.

To begin, preheat your oven to 200°c (gas mark 6) and brush the salmon fillets with 1 tbsp of olive oil. Place them in the oven to bake for 12-15 minutes until cooked through. Once the salmon is cooked, flake it into small pieces and set aside.

Bring a large pot of salted water to the boil and cook your penne according to packet instructions until al dente.

Meanwhile, heat 1 tsp of olive oil in a large skillet over medium-high heat. Add the shallots or onions and garlic to the skillet and sauté for a few minutes until softened. Add the white wine, cream or crème fraîche, lemon zest, lemon juice and flaked salmon pieces. Simmer gently over low heat for around 5-7 minutes until the sauce has thickened slightly.

To serve, drain the cooked penne and combine with the sauce. Divide into plates and enjoy your delicious creamy salmon pasta!

This delicious recipe is sure to be a hit with all the family - even picky eaters will love it! With only a few simple ingredients, this meal can be prepared in no time at all so why not give it a try tonight? Enjoy!

Peanut Butter And Jelly Wings

Ingredients
13 ounces tart cherry jelly.
1/2 cup natural creamy peanut butter.
2 tablespoons apple cider vinegar.
2 tablespoons cherry juice.
1 teaspoon sriracha.
12 chicken drumettes.
Chopped peanuts.

If you're looking for easy and fast chicken recipes, then these Peanut Butter and Jelly Wings are just what you need! With just a few simple ingredients, you can make this delicious dish in no time. To start, combine tart cherry jelly, natural creamy peanut butter, apple cider vinegar, cherry juice and sriracha in a small bowl. Use a whisk to mix everything together until smooth. Heat the mixture in a saucepan over low heat, stirring occasionally, until it begins to simmer. Once the peanut butter and jelly mixture is ready, take 12 chicken drumettes and marinate them in the mixture for 30 minutes or overnight, depending on your preference.

When you're ready to cook, preheat the oven to 375F. Place the chicken drumettes on a greased baking sheet and bake for 20-25 minutes, turning them halfway through. Once they're golden brown and cooked through, take them out of the oven and brush with more of the peanut butter and jelly mixture. Sprinkle with chopped peanuts and serve with a side of your favorite dipping sauce. Enjoy!

Shrimp Pasta

Shrimp Alfredo pasta is a delicious and easy recipe to make for kids. It's quick, delicious, and full of flavor! To start, you'll need to gather all the necessary ingredients: Fettuccine pasta, shrimp (I used frozen raw 31-40 count per pound size shrimp; you can use smaller or larger), butter (unsalted), cream cheese (for added texture and tangy taste), heavy cream, chicken broth (for added flavor), garlic, and Parmesan cheese.

Once you have all of the ingredients ready to go, start by cooking the fettuccine pasta according to package instructions. Once cooked, drain and set aside. In a large skillet or pan, heat butter over medium-high heat. Add the shrimp to the skillet and cook for 3-5 minutes or until they turn pink. Next, add in the garlic and sauté for 2 minutes. Add in cream cheese, heavy cream, and chicken broth and mix everything together until well combined. Lastly, add in the cooked fettuccine pasta and stir for 1-2 minutes until everything is well incorporated. Serve the delicious Shrimp Alfredo pasta with a generous helping of freshly grated Parmesan cheese. Enjoy!

This delicious Shrimp Alfredo pasta recipe is sure to please the whole family, kids included! It's an easy and delicious way to show your family how much you care. Plus, it's a great way to teach kids how to cook delicious recipes for themselves. So what are you waiting for? Give this delicious Shrimp Alfredo pasta recipe a try today!

Air Fryer Chicken Meatballs

Into a large mixing bowl, add ground chicken, egg, bread crumbs, parmesan cheese, salt, pepper, garlic powder, onion powder, paprika, olive oil and parsley and mix until combined. No, take a heaping tablespoon from the chicken mixture and shape it into a ball.

Next, place the chicken meatballs in the air fryer basket and set to 375°F for 12-15 minutes flipping halfway through. This healthy recipe is an easy and fast way to make delicious, low budget meals! You can top these chicken meatballs over pasta or a salad for a complete meal. With air frying, you don't have to worry about the oil or the mess. No need to stand over a hot stove, just preheat and enjoy healthy eating in no time! You can also try this recipe with ground turkey or beef for even more delicious variations. Air frying has revolutionized healthy cooking; easy, fast and healthy recipes are now achievable at home without sacrificing taste. Try this easy air fryer chicken meatballs recipe and enjoy healthy eating today!

The end result: delicious, healthy air fryer chicken meatballs that are an easy and fast way to make low budget meals. With just a few ingredients and the air fryer, you can have healthy meals on the table in no time. Enjoy!

Pesto Quesadillas

If you're looking for vegetarian recipes for kids that are both healthy and delicious, try making these pesto quesadillas! Perfectly cheesy and packed with flavour, they'll become a family favourite in no time.

To make the pesto quesadillas, start by thinly slicing one roma tomato and gathering 3/4 cup of fresh baby spinach. Add 1/4 cup of vegan pesto to the vegetables; if desired, adjust this amount to suit your taste preferences. Next, add 1/2 cup of vegan mozzarella shreds (we recommend Follow Your Heart or Miyokos) as well as 1/4 cup of optional vegan feta crumbles. Place all of the ingredients onto two large tortillas (gluten-free if desired).

Once all of the ingredients are in place, carefully fold the tortillas over and press down to secure the ingredients. Preheat a skillet over medium heat and lightly grease with oil or vegan butter. Place the quesadilla onto the hot skillet and cook for 1-2 minutes on each side until golden brown. Finally, slice into wedges and serve warm!

Your vegetarian kids will love these delicious pesto quesadillas! Enjoy as a main dish, healthy lunchbox treat, or snack. Bon appetite!

Potato Soup

Ingredients

8 slices thin bacon, cut into 1-inch pieces
1 medium onion, diced
2 medium carrots, scrubbed clean and diced
2 stalks celery, diced
4 small russet potatoes, peeled and diced
8 cups low-sodium chicken or vegetable broth
3 tablespoons all-purpose flour
1 cup milk

Instructions for preparing Potato Soup:

In a large pot, cook the bacon over medium heat until crispy, about 5-7 minutes. Remove the bacon with a slotted spoon and set aside. Reserve 2 tablespoons of the bacon fat in the pot.

Add the diced onion, carrots, and celery to the pot and cook until the vegetables are soft and the onion is translucent, about 5-7 minutes.

Stir in the diced potatoes and the chicken or vegetable broth. Bring the soup to a boil, then reduce the heat and simmer until the potatoes are tender, about 20-25 minutes.

In a separate bowl, whisk together the flour and milk until smooth. Stir the flour mixture into the soup and cook until the soup has thickened, about 5-7 minutes.

Return the cooked bacon to the pot and stir to combine. Season the soup with salt and pepper, to taste.

Serve the soup hot, garnished with freshly chopped parsley or green onions, if desired.

Enjoy your delicious and comforting Potato Soup!

Chicken Fajitas

Here is a list of ingredients for chicken fajitas:
- 1 pound boneless, skinless chicken breasts or thighs, sliced into thin strips
- 2 bell peppers (any color), sliced
- 1 large onion, sliced
- 3 tablespoons lime juice
- 2 tablespoons olive oil
- 2 teaspoons chili powder
- 1 teaspoon paprika
- 1 teaspoon cumin
- 1 teaspoon garlic powder
- Salt and pepper, to taste
- 8-10 flour or corn tortillas
- Optional toppings: shredded cheese, sour cream, avocado, salsa, fresh cilantro, etc.

Instructions:
1. In a large bowl, mix together the lime juice, olive oil, chili powder, paprika, cumin, garlic powder, salt, and pepper.
2. Add the chicken, bell peppers, and onions to the bowl and toss to coat with the marinade. Let marinate for at least 30 minutes, or up to 2 hours.
3. Heat a large skillet or griddle over high heat. Add the marinated chicken and vegetables to the skillet, and cook for 5-7 minutes, until the chicken is cooked through and the vegetables are tender.
4. Warm the tortillas in the microwave or on a griddle.
5. To assemble the fajitas, place a few spoonfuls of the chicken and vegetables mixture onto a tortilla, and top with your favorite toppings. Roll up the tortilla and enjoy!

Hawaiian Pork Chops

Here's a list of ingredients for making Hawaiian pork chops:

4 thick pork chops
Salt and pepper, to taste
1/2 cup brown sugar
1/4 cup soy sauce
1 can pineapple rings in juice (reserve the juice)
1 tablespoon onion powder
1 tablespoon garlic powder
1 teaspoon ground ginger

Instructions:

Season the pork chops with salt and pepper on both sides.

In a large bowl, whisk together the brown sugar, soy sauce, reserved pineapple juice, onion powder, garlic powder, and ground ginger to make the marinade.

Place the seasoned pork chops in a large, shallow dish and pour the marinade over the chops, making sure they are well coated.

Cover the dish with plastic wrap and marinate the pork chops in the refrigerator for at least 30 minutes or up to 4 hours.

Preheat the oven to 375°F (190°C).

Remove the pork chops from the marinade and place them in a single layer in a baking dish. Reserve the marinade.

Arrange the pineapple rings around the pork chops.

Bake the pork chops for 25-30 minutes, or until the internal temperature reaches 145°F (63°C). Baste the chops with the reserved marinade several times during cooking.

Serve the pork chops hot, garnished with the baked pineapple rings. Enjoy!

Chinese Pork Rice Fried

Here's a list of ingredients for traditional Chinese pork fried rice:

Cooked white rice (leftover rice is best)
Pork, diced
Scrambled egg
Green onions (scallions), chopped
Soy sauce
Oyster sauce
Hoisin sauce (optional)
Sesame oil (optional)
Vegetable oil or peanut oil, for frying

Instructions:

Heat a large wok or frying pan over high heat. Add oil and swirl to coat the pan.

Add the diced pork and stir-fry for 2-3 minutes, until browned and crispy.

Add the scrambled egg to the pan and stir to combine with the pork. Cook for another minute, until the egg is fully cooked.

Add the cooked rice to the pan and use a spatula to break up any clumps. Stir-fry for 2-3 minutes, until the rice is heated through and coated with the sauces.

Add the green onions and stir to combine.

Drizzle a small amount of soy sauce, oyster sauce, and hoisin sauce over the top of the fried rice, to taste. Stir well to distribute the sauces evenly.

Drizzle a small amount of sesame oil over the top, if desired. Stir to combine.

Serve the pork fried rice hot, garnished with additional chopped green onions, if desired. Enjoy!

Lemon Butter Fish

Ingredients lemon butterfish

1 lb white fish, about four 4-oz fillets- I used halibut.
1 1/2 tbsp olive oil.
1 tsp paprika.
1 tsp garlic powder.
1/2 tsp salt.
1/2 tsp black pepper.
Lemon Butter Sauce.
1/4 cup butter.

Instructions:

Preheat your oven to 400°F (200°C). Line a large baking sheet with parchment paper or lightly grease with cooking spray.

In a small bowl, mix together the olive oil, paprika, garlic powder, salt, and pepper.

Place the fish fillets on the prepared baking sheet. Brush both sides of the fish with the olive oil mixture.

Bake for 10-12 minutes, or until the fish is opaque and flakes easily with a fork.

While the fish is baking, make the lemon butter sauce. In a small saucepan, melt the butter over medium heat. Add freshly squeezed lemon juice, minced garlic, and dried herbs (such as thyme or basil) to taste. Stir to combine and cook for 1-2 minutes until the sauce is heated through.

Remove the baked fish from the oven and transfer to a serving platter. Spoon the lemon butter sauce over the top of each fish fillet.

Serve the lemon butter fish hot with your favorite side dishes, such as roasted vegetables or a fresh salad.

Enjoy your delicious and flavorful lemon butter fish!

Chicken Parmigiana:

Ingredients for

2 large, skinless chicken breasts, halved through the middle
2 eggs, beaten
75g breadcrumbs
75g parmesan, grated
1 tbsp olive oil
2 garlic cloves, crushed
Half a 690ml jar of passata
1 tsp caster sugar

Instructions for preparing Chicken Parmigiana:

Preheat the oven to 200°C (400°F). Line a baking sheet with parchment paper.

Place the beaten eggs in a shallow dish and set aside. In another shallow dish, mix together the breadcrumbs and grated parmesan.

Dip each chicken breast into the beaten eggs, then coat with the breadcrumb mixture, pressing the breadcrumbs firmly onto the chicken.

Heat the olive oil in a large skillet over medium heat. Add the coated chicken breasts and cook until browned on both sides, about 3-5 minutes per side.

Transfer the chicken to the prepared baking sheet and bake in the preheated oven for 15-20 minutes, or until the chicken is cooked through and the breadcrumbs are golden brown.

While the chicken is baking, prepare the sauce. In a small saucepan, heat the garlic in the remaining olive oil until fragrant. Stir in the passata and caster sugar and cook until heated through.

Serve the chicken parmigiana topped with the warm tomato sauce, with a side of pasta or vegetables, if desired. Enjoy!

Potato Broccoli Frittata

Ingredients for 6 Servings

1 1/2 cups cubed potatoes
2 cups coarsely chopped broccoli florets
1 tablespoon olive oil
1/2 cup coarsely chopped onion
1 teaspoon McCormick Oregano Leaves
1 teaspoon McCormick Whole Rosemary Leaves, finely crushed
1 teaspoon McCormick Whole Thyme Leaves
8 large eggs
1/4 teaspoon salt
1/4 teaspoon black pepper
1/4 cup grated Parmesan cheese

Instructions for preparing Potato and Broccoli Frittata:

Preheat oven to 400°F. In a large skillet, heat the olive oil over medium heat. Add the potatoes, broccoli, onion, oregano, rosemary, and thyme. Cook for 10 to 12 minutes or until the vegetables are tender and lightly browned, stirring occasionally.

In a large bowl, whisk the eggs, salt, pepper, and Parmesan cheese together until well combined. Stir in the cooked vegetable mixture.

Pour the egg mixture back into the skillet. Cook over medium heat until the bottom is set and the top is almost set, about 5 minutes.

Place the skillet in the oven and bake for 10 minutes or until the frittata is set and lightly browned on top.

Remove the frittata from the oven and let it cool for 5 minutes. Slide the frittata onto a serving platter and cut into wedges.

Enjoy your delicious and nutritious Potato and Broccoli Frittata! Serve it warm or at room temperature, as a tasty and complete meal.

I want to take a moment to express my heartfelt gratitude for your recent purchase of my recipe book. As a passionate food lover, nothing makes me happier than sharing my favorite recipes with others. Your decision to invest in my book not only supports my dream, but also shows your commitment to expanding your culinary horizons.

I sincerely hope that the recipes in the book will inspire you to try new things and add some excitement to your meals.

Thank you again for your support and for being a part of this journey with me. I hope my book will bring you many happy and delicious moments in the kitchen.

www.ingramcontent.com/pod-product-compliance
Lightning Source LLC
Chambersburg PA
CBHW041151110526
44590CB00027B/4192